GREEK MYTHOLOGY

FOR KIDS

CHARLES MCKINNEY

DR. HISTORY

GREEK MYTHOLOGY

History of Most Influential Greek Mythology

FOR KIDS

CHARLES MCKINNEY

DR. HISTORY

Don't Forget Your Free Bonus Downloads!

As our way of saying thank you, we've included in every purchase bonus gift downloads. If you've enjoyed reading this book, please consider leaving a review.

Or Scan Your Phone to open QR code

Greek Mythology:

History of Most Influential Greek Mythology for Kids

TABLE OF CONTENTS

INTRODUCTION

"A society grows great when old men plant trees whose shade they know they shall never sit in."

– A Greek Proverb

The stories of Greek Mythology have been passed down from generation to generation, from century to century, and from person to person. Greek Mythology is mostly known as stories. But where did Greek Mythology come from? How were these stories come up with, and how were they spread? What was so important about them? Today, those of the modern age believe these stories to be just that; stories. However, there was a time centuries ago when Greek Myths were not myths. They were a religion. They were what stories from the Bible are to Christians. They were what passages from the Quran are to Muslims.

Greek Mythology covers stories of how the earth was formed, created, and ruled by the Titans and then later the gods and goddesses of Olympus. There are also stories of the changing of the seasons, historical events like the Trojan War, and many others that could explain major points in history connected to their beliefs and culture.

Today, history is easily documented through the use of writing and technology. Back then, however, documenting historical events was not as simple. The use of illustrations and art was the only way historical events could be documented, and because of that, no one can really know for sure if these events were just "myths" as civilization knows them to be.

From the creation of the earth, to Zeus's many children, their exploits, and the many creatures of Greek Mythology will all be covered today. The connection of Greek Mythology to historical events will also be mentioned and discussed. Along with that, stories of how these Greek Myths were spread and the methods of those living in Ancient Greece to share these stories will also be discussed, such as pottery and sculpting.

After Greek Mythology was so heavily relied upon as a way of living and as a religion, the fall of which was inevitable. The conquering of Greece by the Roman Empire was only the beginning of the end. The conversion and, later, the destruction of temples and artifacts and changing of religions and cultural ways are just some of the reasons Greek Mythology is as we know it today. Though Greek Mythology is considered to be fiction, no one can deny the influence it has had on many civilizations.

IN THE BEGINNING...

The columns of this building are built to depict how the Titan, Atlas, is carrying the weight of the world on his shoulders. Atlas was sentenced to hold up the Earth for eternity.

There are different beliefs as to how the world and humankind started, most of these stemming from religious or theological practices. In Christianity, it is believed that the world started when God said, "Let there be light," and thus started the story that is known to be the seven days of creation and rest. Islam has their own version of the story of how the world was created, believing also that one "god" or one "all-powerful being" created the entire universe.

In Hinduism, it is believed that the creation of the world was thanks to the "Trimurti," which is what they believe to be the "Ultimate Divine Reality" that is made up of "Brahma," "Vishnu," and "Shiva." According to their belief, Brahma is the creator of everything, Vishnu is the being responsible for preserving what has already been created, and Vishnu is the being that is responsible for the destruction.

Other than religious beliefs, there are also theories about the universe's origin, the most popular theory being "The Big Bang Theory." In this theory, scientists believe that the entire universe started from just a single molecular point that expanded and stretched to form the Universe as we know it today, even believing that it is still expanding and stretching.

Many of these theories and religions are still being believed and practiced today. There are also many theological beliefs and practices that were abandoned many years ago. These beliefs are now known today as "mythology." A common branch of mythology that plenty of people still read and learn about is Greek Mythology.

Like in many theological beliefs of how the Universe was formed, the stories of Greek Mythology believed the same: that, in the beginning, the universe had no form. Though matter existed, it seemed to have no shape or form and was only dark. This was called "Chaos." Later, other gods and goddesses started to appear or take form. The first to appear was Gaea, the goddess of the Earth. Next was her son, Uranus, who was considered to be the personification of The Sky. From Gaea and Uranus, the Titans were born.

There were many Titans, but the most important one was Cronus. He castrated and killed his father, Uranus, in order to help his mother and then became the chief of the Titans. He married his sister, Rhea, and together they birthed the Olympian gods. Before the birth of Zeus and his siblings, Cronus had heard of a prophecy saying he would be overthrown from his position of power by his own children and killed, just like he did to his father. To prevent this prophecy from coming to fruition, he ate his children every time they were born. Rhea gave birth to their sixth child, Zeus, in secret in order to protect him and had him taken away to Crete. She tricked Cronus by wrapping Zeus's clothes around a stone and having Cronus eat it, making him believe he had devoured his sixth and final child. Later on, Cronus vomited the children he had previously eaten. The five children and Zeus all led a 10-year war that led to the defeat of Cronus.

After Cronus's defeat, Zeus and his five siblings, Hestia, Demeter, Hera, Hades, and Poseidon, decided they would rule. Zeus married Hera and divided the world among himself and his brothers. Zeus was to rule the Sky, Poseidon was to rule the Seas, and Hades was to rule the Underworld. Zeus had many children with Hera and other goddesses. These other children were Athena, Apollo, Artemis, Hermes, Aphrodite, Ares, and Hephaestus. Zeus, four of his siblings, and his seven children are said to live in the Heavens, which is said to be at the Summit of Mount Olympus, and thus they were named "The Twelve Olympians." Hades, who decided he was to rule the Underworld, was not counted in the twelve.

It was from this series of events that mankind was created. One of the Titans, Prometheus, did not fight against Zeus and the other gods during the war. In return, Zeus spared him and gave him the task of creating mankind. He used mud to shape the men, and it was Athena who breathed life into them. And from then, mankind was born.

Fun Fact:

At the time of Ancient Greece, the Greeks worshipped the gods and goddesses of Olympus as a religion and way of living. At the time, they believed that mankind was made out of clay and had to have life breathed into them in order for them to come alive. Nowadays, most of them practice Christianity instead.

Fun Fact:

Greek Mythology is a branch of mythology many find themselves familiar with due to modern-day adaptations and retellings. Some popular adaptations are Disney's 1997 film, "Hercules," the 2004 film, "Troy" which was directed by Wolfgang Peterson and written by David Benioff, and, most recently, "The Percy Jackson" series, a series of middle-grade fantasy novels of a retelling of Greek Mythology written by Rick Riordan targeted towards children and young adults.

Trivia Questions:

1. What is the name of matter that has no shape or form and is only dark?
2. Who is the Goddess of the Earth?
3. Who is the son of the Goddess of the Earth?
4. Who defeated Cronus?
5. Who is the God of the Underworld?

Answers:

1. What is the name of matter that has no shape or form and is only dark? **Chaos**

2. Who is the Goddess of the Earth? **Gaea**

3. Who is the son of the Goddess of the Earth? **Uranus**

4. Who defeated Cronus? **Zeus**

5. Who is the God of the Underworld? **Hades**

THE CREATURES OF GREEK MYTHOLOGY

Along with the gods and Titans, there were many other species and creatures in Greek Mythology. There were the cyclops who were born from the Titans, centaurs, gorgons, satyrs, and so many more.

One of the oldest creatures from Greek Mythology are the Cyclops. The Cyclops are gigantic divine beings with immense strength and power and only have a single eye on the center of their forehead. In Greek Mythology, it is unclear just where the cyclops came from. There are two versions wherein the physical attributes of the cyclops are the same but are different in terms of behavior and origin. These two versions came from the two most famous Greek poets, Hesiod and Homer.

In Hesiod's version, the three Cyclops, Arges, Steropes, and Brontes, were born shortly after the Titans and are also children of Uranus and Gaea. According to Hesiod's

"Theogony," he says that the three Cyclops are all also known as "Bright," "Thunderer," and "Lightener." According to Hesiod's Theogony, these three Cyclops are master blacksmiths. It is said that Cronus, who had previously had the three Cyclops imprisoned in Tartarus, was freed by Zeus during the Titan War. Because Zeus freed them, the three Cyclops sided with Zeus during the war, even forging his famous Thunderbolt. They also forged Poseidon's Trident and Hades' Helmet of Invisibility. After the war ended, the Cyclops went under Hephaestus's care and stayed in Sicily's forges. They continued to make Thunderbolts for Zeus and even made Artemis's armor, Apollo's Chariot, and many more weapons and forged items.

In Homer's version of the Cyclops, his physical description of them is similar to that of Hesiod's. The main difference is in their attitudes and way of living. In "The Odyssey," he writes that the Cyclops is an unintelligent, violent, and cannibalistic race who live as shepherds in Sicily. The specific Cyclops that Homer writes about is Polyphemus, the son of the god Poseidon, and Thoösa, a nymph. Though both poets gave similar descriptions, there is no direct confirmation as to how the two poets came up with the versions of the Cyclops that they portrayed in their works.

Other famous species from Greek Mythology are the Centaurs. The Centaurs are half man and half horse. From the waist up, they have the appearance of a man. And then, from the waist down, they have the form of a horse from the neck down. In early versions of Greek Mythology, it is said that the Centaurs were a violent species, considered by most as savages.

However, though Centaurs are known to be wild and unruly, a well-known Centaur who is spoken about in many stories in Greek Mythology is Chiron. Chiron was a wise centaur. He was educated and civilized, but he was also known for being a healer, oracle, and astrologer. Thanks to his wisdom and knowledge, he was able to teach a lot of famous heroes from Greek Mythology. Some of these heroes include Achilles, known for being a near undefeatable warrior during the Trojan War, and Jason, who is mostly known for his quest to find the Golden Fleece.

Another example of a famous creature from Greek Mythology are the Sirens. According to mythology, the Sirens were fathered by the river god, Achelous and one of the nine Muses. Which Muse, however, was the question. Many people guess it might be either Terpsichore, Melpomene, or Calliope.

Sirens are half human, and half bird. They are depicted as vicious, man-eating creatures who lure in their pray by singing to them and hypnotizing them to believe they are beautiful women, and then once they are in their grasp, the victims are eaten. In Homer's "The Odyssey," Odyssey and his comrades are to sail past an island known for having Sirens, so Odysseus has the men tie him to the mast of the ship and then instructs the men to stuff their ears with wax in order to block out the singing of the Sirens.

The Cyclops, Centaurs, and the Sirens are just a select few from a wide array of creatures in Greek Mythology. There are so many more unique and interesting creatures in Greek Mythology, all living in different parts of the world. Some live in Olympus, some live on land, and there are some who even live in the Underworld.

Fun Fact:

Today, most people consider "sirens" and "mermaids" to be synonymous with one another, but both creatures, though they do have similarities, are mostly different. The only similarities they do have are that they both dwell in the sea and are both half human and half creature. Mermaids are half human, half fish and are (usually) portrayed as peaceful and loving creatures, while sirens are vicious and half-human and half-bird.

Fun Fact:

There are many versions of where Centaurs came from. In one version, the Centaurs were born from Ixion, a son of Ares, mating with the Magnesian Mares. In another version, they claim that Zeus had transformed into a horse and mated with Dia, the wife of Ixion, in order to create the Centaurs.

Match Phrases:

Centaurs	Giants with one eye on their forehead.
Homer	Wild and unruly half-horse and half-men creatures.
Siren	A wise and educated half-horse and half-man who tutored many heroes.
Chiron	Half-human and half-bird man-eating sea creatures.
Cyclops	Writer of the "Odyssey."

Answer:	
Cyclops	Giants with one eye on their forehead.
Centaurs	Wild and unruly half-horse and half-men creatures.
Chiron	A wise and educated half-horse and half-man who tutored many heroes.
Siren	Half-human and half-bird man-eating sea creatures.
Homer	Writer of the "Odyssey."

ZEUS'S MANY AFFAIRS AND THEIR FAMOUS OFFSPRING

This is a statue of the goddess, Aphrodite. This statue can be found in the Canakkale Archaeological Museum in Turkey.

Many know Zeus to be the God of the Skies and the Father of the Gods and Men. He is known to be the most powerful god of Olympus, his weapon of choice being his Lightning Bolts made by Hephaestus and the Cyclops. It is a common misconception, however, that Zeus and the other gods and goddesses included in the Twelve Olympians are all siblings. As a matter of fact, only four of them are Zeus's siblings, and Zeus's fifth sibling is Hades, the god of the Underworld, and is not counted as one of the Twelve Olympians. So where did the Twelve Olympians' other six gods and goddesses come from?

Zeus married his sister, Hera, the goddess of marriage and women. The most famous account of how their relationship started was how Zeus transformed himself into a cuckoo and sat on Hera's lap whilst she was on the way to Mount Thornax. She took pity on the bird and took care of him, and then Zeus transformed himself back and wooed her. It was with Hera that Zeus fathered two other Olympian gods, Ares, the god of war, and Hephaestus, the god of blacksmiths and volcanoes. It is said that Hera found Hephaestus so ugly that she threw him off her balcony, only for him to survive, live, and grow up. Hera was also infamous for her jealousy. Though she remained faithful to Zeus, Zeus did not give her that same courtesy. In fact, Zeus was infamous for having many affairs and possibly fathering the majority of the gods, goddesses, and other mythological heroes and creatures.

Many sources have different opinions on the exact order of

Zeus's affairs, but we will start with the birth of the rest of the gods and goddesses of the Twelve Olympians. According to Hesiod's "Theogony," Zeus's first affair was with Metis. It is said that it was with Metis that Zeus fathered Athena, famously known as the goddess of wisdom and war. Athena's birth is one of those most known in Greek Mythology due to the unique way she was birthed. According to Greek Mythology, she was born from Zeus's forehead, fully formed and in complete battle armor.

He then had a relationship with the Titan goddess, Leto. Leto then gave birth to two of Zeus's children, Apollo and Artemis. Apollo is the god of music and the sun. On the other hand, Artemis is the goddess of the hunt and the moon. In mythology, they say Leto had to find a place to hide in order to give birth away from the all-seeing eyes of Hera, whom she knew would punish her for lying with her husband.

Much later, Zeus fathered Hermes. Hermes's mother was Maia, one of the seven Pleiades who cared for Zeus's other son, Dionysus, when he was a baby. Zeus also fathered the goddess Aphrodite, the goddess of beauty, with Dione, a goddess who is also an oracle who is able to predict prophecies.

Other than the rest of the Twelve Olympians, Zeus is also famous for fathering other famous humans from Greek Mythology. One of them is Helen of Troy. Helen of Troy's mother is believed to be Leda, a Spartan Queen. Zeus had a secret affair with her that resulted in the birth of Helen. Helen was known to be the most beautiful woman in the world. She was initially married to King Menelaus of Sparta but was later seduced by Paris, who had previously made a deal with Aphrodite that she would give him "the most beautiful woman in the world," Helen. King Menelaus of Sparta retaliated by waging war upon Troy. This was the start of the "Trojan War."

Lastly, there is Hercules. His mother is Alcmene, a human woman. As an adult, he married Megara, the daughter of King Creon. After Heracles got married and had children, Hera enacted her revenge on Zeus by inducing a fit of madness in Heracles. It was during this rage that Heracles killed Megara and their children. King Eurystheus, his enemy, ordered Heracles to complete ten tasks in order to exempt him from the crime of killing his children. Zeus also added the promise of immortality. Heracles completed these tasks and later even joined the Spartans in fighting against Troy in the Trojan War.

There are many more heroes and creatures fathered by Zeus in Greek Mythology. The ones mentioned here were just a few. Many of the characters in these myths are most likely to have some type of relation to Zeus. Reading up about Zeus is already a big chunk of Greek Mythology.

Fun Fact:

Heracles is the demigod hero most people know about today. That is due to the Disney Animated Film, "Hercules" that came out in 1997. The film is not an accurate depiction of Heracles' story. Instead, it took major elements from Heracles' story and turned it into a more child-appropriate story. A major change the film made was making Hera his mother.

— · — · — · —

Fun Fact:

After King Menaleus declared war against Troy, he deployed thousands of ships to head towards Troy and start the Trojan War. It was well known that Helen was a great beauty, which is why Paris wanted her in the first place. It was because of this event that Helen was dubbed "the face that launched a thousand ships."

Fill in the blanks to complete the story:

1. _____ to be the God of the Skies and the Father of the Gods and Men.

2. Zeus married his sister, _____, the goddess of marriage and women.

3. It was with Metis that Zeus fathered _______, the goddess of wisdom and war.

4. _______ is the god of music and the sun.

5. Helen was known to be the most __________ woman in the world.

Answers:

1. **Zeus** to be the God of the Skies and the Father of the Gods and Men.

2. Zeus married his sister, **Hera,** the goddess of marriage and women.

3. It was with Metis that Zeus fathered **Athena,** the goddess of wisdom and war.

4. **Apollo** is the god of music and the sun.

5. Helen was known to be the most **beautiful** woman in the world.

GREEK MYTHOLOGY WAS A RELIGION

This is a statue of the goddess, Athena, made by Alan LeQuire. It is displayed in Nashville, Tennessee. This statue is a replica of the lost statue of Athena that used to be in the Parthenon. LeQuire used descriptions founded by archaeologists to create his work.

Greek Mythology is known today in modern society as fictional stories passed down through time, preserved through the verbal communication of storytelling and play presented by the Ancient Greeks. The Greek myths most known are the stories pertaining to the Twelve Olympians. The Twelve Olympians consist of Zeus, Poseidon, and Hades, and their siblings and children.

Citizens of Ancient Greece used the stories of the gods and goddesses of Olympus and many other minor gods to explain the ways of nature and natural phenomena, historical events, political decisions, and human nature. Essentially, the Ancient Greeks considered these stories as their religion and as a basis and reasoning for everything around them. Stories such as Persephone's stay in the Underworld with Hades every six months to symbolize the changing of seasons, Poseidon striking his trident were believed to be the causes of storms, earthquakes, and volcanic eruptions, and even Zeus throwing his thunderbolts around in anger were believed to also be the cause of storms. Even dying was connected to Greek Mythology. It was believed that, upon dying, your soul would be brought to the Underworld, ruled by the God, Hades.

Greek Mythology has a deity connected or assigned to at least one aspect of life. Zeus, Poseidon, and Hades are the gods of the Sky, the Sea, and the Underworld, respectively. Aphrodite was the goddess of beauty, and Hermes, the Messenger, was the god of travel.

Greek Mythology also includes its own version of how

mankind came to be, including an origin story of the gods and goddesses of Olympus and how they were born. Most of them are actually siblings or are related to each other in some kind of way. For example, though Zeus and Hera are famously known to be husband and wife, they are also brother and sister.

Temples were built to honor the gods and goddesses where citizens could come to make offerings and ask for blessings and guidance from them; towns were named after them – the most famous being "Athens," named after the goddess, "Athena" – and people feared the power of these powerful beings. As a religion, the theology of Greek Myths was a polytheistic one.

The gods and goddesses were thought to be all-powerful beings, but humans still thought of them with human characteristics, humanizing them and using them as representations for people such as politicians and human relationships. Zeus and Hera were used as an example of romantic relationships. Zeus was infamous for having relationships with other women, whether they be other (minor) goddesses or even humans. Hera, known to be the Goddess of Women, Marriage, and Childbirth, did not approve of this. Zeus and Hera, the King and Queen of the Gods, were thought to be the perfect and most powerful couple, yet they were also used to represent the stereotype of the husband being unfaithful and the wife being left alone to feel betrayed.

The stories shared about the gods and goddesses were often used as a model for practical advice on daily living, the stories presenting themselves almost like a life lesson.

Though these stories are no longer thought of as true events or even religion, there are many who still use the stories of Greek Mythology as references and inspiration for their daily lives.

Fun Fact: .

The story of Icarus and Daedalus is a good example of a story that gives practical and moral advice. In the story, Daedalus, an amazing craftsman and architect created wings made of branches and wax so that he and his son, Icarus, would be able to fly away and escape from their imprisonment in the Labyrinth. He instructed Icarus not to fly too close to the sun, for it could melt the wax and destroy the wings. In his excitement at being able to fly, Icarus failed to heed Daedalus's warning and fell to his death. This is a story that teaches the listener to be mindful of hubris.

Fun Fact:

Artemis and Apollo's story is about familial relationships, Artemis was the goddess of the moon, hunt, and chastity. Apollo was the god of the sun, light, healing, and art (including poetry and music). With both representing totally opposite elements of the world, the two are known to go head-to-head, rivaling each other. Not to mention, both also prefer archery as their weapon of choice.

Fill in the Blanks to Complete the Story

Daedalus and his son, ______, were trapped in the center of the _________. To escape, the two of them would have to fly out. Daedalus created wings made of branches and ___ so that they could fly. Daedalus instructed his son not to fly too close to the ___; however his instructions were ignored, and his son ____ to his death.

Answer:

Daedalus and his son, **Icarus,** were trapped in the center of the **Labyrinth.** To escape, the two of them would have to fly out. Daedalus created wings made of branches and **wax** so that they could fly. Daedalus instructed his son not to fly too close to the **sun;** however his instructions were ignored, and his son **fell** to his death.

THE STORYTELLING OF THE MYTHS

This picture shows Greek Pottery in a museum display. Many of the pieces shown have stories painted on them.

Today, things such as the internet, books, voice recordings, video recordings, photographs, and many other mediums of communication exist. Stories could be told consistently and accurately over and over again without the worry of the original version being muddled or embellished. During the time of Ancient Greece, however, there were no such mediums that could assist the citizens of the time with storytelling. The only way stories, news, and information could be spread around was through oral communication.

The spreading of these stories was said to have most probably been done by Minoan and Mycenaean bards. Bards are storytellers who usually express their tales through traditional storytelling, or they could compose their story into a poem or song and then perform it for a crowd. Bards tend to share their stories in public spaces, or there could be times when they could be hired by merchants, noblemen, or royalty to share these stories at a feast or banquet.

Bards, having to use these stories to entertain, may sometimes add an embellishment or two to the story they're telling or could exaggerate the story in order to keep their audiences' attention. Usually, bards experience the topics they sing songs or tell stories about firsthand, stories that are known today are known to have a bard present in the actual event. In the story of the Odyssey, a well-known Greek mythology story about Odysseus and his journey home after the Trojan War, it is known that there were two bards, Phemius and Demodocus, present with him on his journey home.

So, because these stories could have been edited slightly to entice more people to listen to these bards, it is possible that the version the audience is told is not exactly fully accurate. Then from the people who were able to watch and listen to these bards, they could pass these stories on to anyone who might want to listen, editing the story even more. With each interpretation of the story is told, not only are they keeping in mind the version of the story the bards told, but they are also telling the story according to their own memory, which may or may not get everything correctly. So, whenever someone tells the story, it is possible that a whole new version of the myth has been told, even with the smallest changes.

Around the 8th century BCE, these stories that were originally passed down verbally from person to person, then later on to pieces of art, were finally put on paper, or papyrus, which they used back then. The Egyptians started this practice, which the Greeks later adapted. Though previously poems were recited by bards only verbally, it was during this time that poems were then written down. The poems most known today were those written by Hesiod and Homer. Homer is most famous for his poem "The Iliad." The poem tells of what transpired during the Trojan War. Another poem Homer is famous for is "The Odyssey." This is a poem about what transpired after "The Iliad," specifically, the journey home of the hero Odysseus after fighting in the Trojan War. Hesiod was another famous poet. He was most known for his two works, "Theogony" and "Works and Days." "Theogony" tells the story of the gods and their origin. "Works and Days," on the other hand, talks about the origin of humankind based on the pre-existing stories of Greek Mythology. Another work of his that is not as well known is the "Catalogue of Women." This poem dictates the women who had relations with gods and then birthed heroes in Greek Mythology. Though Hesiod's works were only written down years after his death, his works are still known today.

This went on probably until the Ancient Greeks started documenting historical events in a physical and concrete manner. Some of the first methods of documentation were done through art. This practice became widespread around the 8th century BCE. Pottery is the practice of using clay to form items such as vases, bowls, and plates that would then be dried or baked to permanently retain the shape it was formed into. Sometimes, while the clay is still drying after being formed, artists would carve or engrave designs on the piece. Other times, they would paint designs on the piece. These designs are usually depictions of stories or events that had transpired at the time.

Another method of documentation through art was through sculptures. Sculptors had many options for making these sculptures. They could use wood, stone, limestone, and many others. However, the material most of these sculptors have chosen seemed to be marble, which is what you would find in most museums today. Sculptures of scenes from these myths were later on used to decorate public spaces such as the Parthenon and the Temple of Zeus. The most important sculpture in the Parthenon was the Statue of Athena. It stands 12 meters high and is made of ivory and gold.

The downside to these methods of documentation was that they could be open for interpretation. Because you would only be able to decorate vases with illustrations to depict a story, and sculptures can only be in one pose, these methods are not exactly able to tell the viewer the full story.

Fun Fact:

The Parthenon was built from 447 BC to 432 BC. However, the decision to have the Parthenon be the home of the 12-meter-high statue of Athena was only made in 438 BC. When Greece was conquered by the Byzantines in the 6th century AD, Christianity became the primary religion, and so, like many other Greek temples, the Parthenon was converted into a Christian church. Later, when the Ottoman Empire conquered Greece, they converted it into a mosque. Finally, in 1687, the Parthenon was destroyed by the Christian Holy League.

Fun Fact:

The Met Museum has at least two Greek vases on display in their exhibit. Both of these vases have scenes from Greek Mythology painted on them. One vase depicts the story of Heracles and the twelve trials he was tasked with. Another vase has a battle between the Greeks and the Amazons painted on it.

Match the Poet to Their Work

1. Homer

2. Hesiod

Options: Works and Days, The Iliad, Theogony, The Odyssey, Catalogue of Women

Answers

Homer: The Iliad, The Odyssey

Hesiod: Works and Days, Theogony, Catalogue of Women

GREEK MYTHOLOGY AND THEATER

This is a statue of a Satyr on display in a museum's outdoor area.

Three centuries after the introduction of using pottery and sculptures to spread the stories of the Greek gods and goddesses, a new form of sharing these stories was born. In the 5th century BCE, myths were told through the art of theater. The theater started in Greece around the 6th century BCE. Performers would put up Greek plays, specifically tragedies, to be performed during religious festivals to honor the gods and goddesses. Most of the time, these performances were done in honor of the God Dionysus, more commonly known as the "God of Wine," but with the spread of theater and its use to honor him, he later on, became known to also be the "God of Wine and Theater." Most aspects of theater have also stemmed from religious practices and beliefs in accordance with the stories about Dionysus. An example of this is the term "Satyr," which is a type of play in the theater that focuses on parody. It was given the name "Satyr" because actors would be dressed up as satyrs, the mythological creatures that are half man and half goat, and would dance around on stage, similar to how the stories say the satyrs would follow Dionysus around.

Greek Tragedy is the most common type of theater performed during religious festivals. Its origin remains obscure up to this day. There are many theories, but the most common one is that the practice of performing tragedies stems from rituals that would be performed to worship the gods, specifically in honor of Dionysus, which was where Greek Tragedies originated from. It has been theorized that the practice of "tragodia," a song ritual where they sacrifice goats and wear masks, was the seed of Greek tragedy. In Athens, specifically in the city of Dionysia, they would have a theater competition whenever they would hold their local spring festival in honor of Dionysus. Many citizens from the city would be involved. A city official (the archon) would be the one to pick which plays would be performed and also which male citizens would be the performers. The plays would be judged on the day of the festival by a panel of judges, and the winners would usually receive a type of bronze cauldron, along with honor, recognition, and prestige from festivalgoers.

Plays about Greek myths started being performed around the 5th century BCE. Most of the plays inspired by Greek mythology stories are tragedies. Because, at the time, what we now know as Greek Mythology used to be considered "religion" back then, plays with plots inspired by Greek myths were always treated with solemnity and with respect.

In order to ensure the solemnity of these stories on stage, there were many rules the actors had to follow to make sure that the stories were handled respectfully and carefully. There were two main rules to this; the first was that there was to be no violence on stage. Any act of violence that was to be done, even though it is an act included in the original story, must be done offstage. Another actor or a chorus member would usually then run onstage and narrate the violence that happened away from the audience's view. Another rule they had to follow was to keep to the original story and not make any commentary, especially political commentary, in the play.

"Poets" are what you used to call those who wrote plays for the festivals. Later, they were named "playwrights" instead. The most successful playwrights were Aeschylus, Sophocles, and Euripides. These three playwrights submitted works regularly for the festivals. To this day, the works of these playwrights, most notably Sophocles's "Oedipus Rex," are being read and performed by the general public and have even been considered "required reading" in schools. This goes to show that, though these works were first performed way back in the 5th century BCE, they are works that are still as important and as captivating today as it was back then.

Fun Fact:

"Oedipus Rex" tells the story of a man who grew up to be a king and married the widowed queen of the previous king, only for him to find out at the end of the play that he is actually their son who was given away at birth and that the queen he married, is also his mother. This play became the basis for what is now known as the "Oedipus Complex," meaning having a sexual or romantic desire for a parent of the opposite sex. This play is a lesson on hubris.

Fun Fact:

"Lysistrata" is another famous play written during the time of Ancient Greece. It tells the story of the women of Greece deciding that they would withhold from sexual activities unless their husbands decided to negotiate for peace instead of continuing battle. This was written by Aristophanes sometime toward the end of the war between Athens and Sparta. It is a comedy that was written in the hopes of peace.

Trivia Question:

1. Who was the God of Wine? What did this God later also become the god of?

2. Why was the parodical play given the name "Satyr?"

3. Why were most plays inspired by Greek Myths and tragedies?

4. Why did tragedies have so many rules as to how they should be performed?

5. Why did Aristophanes write Lysistrata?

Answers

1. Dionysus. Theater.

2. It was named such because the actors would be dressed up like satyrs and move around the stage like how the satyrs are said to have followed Dionysus around.

3. Plays inspired by Greek Myths were tragedies because this was their religion back then and needed to be treated with solemnity and respect.

4. Tragedies had many rules because actors needed to make sure they treated the material with solemnity and respect since it was their religion at the time.

5. Aristophanes wrote Lysistrata because he wanted the war between Athens and Sparta to end.

THE FIRST CAUSE OF EXISTENCE

This is a statue of Pan the Satyr kept in Munich, Germany.

The belief of the Ancient Greeks that the world was started by the appearance of Titans and then, later on, was ruled by gods and goddesses went on for centuries. Though circumstances and the involvement of the gods and goddesses were questioned, no one could deny that some stories connected to Greek Mythology actually happened, such as the Trojan War. Up until the 1870s, when Heinrich Schliemann, a German merchant, traveled to Turkey, which was where Troy was estimated to be, and found evidence of the Trojan War, people thought that the Trojan War, just like other stories of Greek Mythology was just that – a myth.

In the 6th century BCE, just as Greek mythology was being spread through theater, philosophers had started to get into science and were looking for a more scientific explanation as to how the earth and mankind were created and originated from, as well as looking into more scientific explanations to natural phenomena, rather than supernatural or mystical reasoning. The philosopher who started this theory was Thales of Miletus. Initially, he did not deny the existence of the gods and goddesses, but he did suggest an order in which the earth was created. Such as how he believed that water was the first element that came into existence. He believed that water was the First Cause of Existence because it was an element that helped mankind live and because you could find water pretty much anywhere in the world. Other than that, another reason he believed it to be water had the ability to take on different forms, such as solidifying as a liquid, and steam when heated. Thales's two followers, Anaximander and Anaximenes, continued his work, but found evidence that perhaps water was not the First Cause of Existence. The philosophers who first started looking into these are called "Pre-Socratic Philosophers," meaning the philosophers before the birth of Socrates. These philosophers studied what they believed to be called the "First Cause of Existence."

It was argued later on by Anaximander that water may not have been the first cause of existence. He believed this to be so because he thought that the first cause would be a cosmic force that would be capable of creating, destroying, and remaking the world.

This study was later on called "Greek Philosophy." The three men, Thales, Anaximander, and Anaximenes, initiated "Greek Philosophy," and then were later on dubbed in history as "Pre-Socratic Philosophers."

Many other followers joined the study to find the First Cause of Existence. Many of them had differing opinions on how the world could have started, but the most common among all of them was that the creation of mankind was not entirely the work of the gods and goddesses of Olympus.

Fun Fact:

Greek Philosophers did not just study reasoning or possible ways the earth was created. A lot of them were scholars and scientists who studied science and mathematics. Archimedes of Syracuse was the first ever mathematician to calculate the value of pi, a mathematical concept that is still being taught and used today.

Fun Fact:

A very famous Greek Philosopher was Aristotle. He was considered to be one of the greatest philosophers, and his knowledge includes biology, chemistry, history, physics, political theory, philosophy itself, and many more. He was most famous for founding "formal logic," a practice adapted into western culture and still used today. He founded his own school in Athens called "The Lyceum." He is also known for being the tutor of Alexander the Great.

True or False:

1. Heinrich Schliemann traveled to Germany, where Troy was estimated to be.

2. Scientists started looking for a more scientific explanation of the earth's creation in the 6th century BCE.

3. The philosopher who came up with the First Cause of Existence was Anaximander.

4. Thales, Anaximander, and Anaximenes were called "Pre-Socratic Philosophers."

5. Aristotle was a student at "The Lyceum."

Answers:

1. **False.** He traveled to Turkey because that was where Troy was estimated to be.

2. **True.**

3. **False.** Thales of Miletus came up with the First Cause of Existence.

4. **True.**

5. **False.** Aristotle was the one who founded "The Lyceum."

THE CONQUERING OF GREECE

In 146 BCE, the Romans, led by Alexander the Great, conquered Greece. After occupying Greece, the Roman Empire made many changes to its culture and way of living. The Romans, known for their luxurious lifestyles, raised taxes to accommodate their tastes. They also had the architecture of most buildings changed to better suit more Roman styles. However, one of the Romans' biggest changes was in their mythology and the story of the Greek gods and goddesses.

Just like the people of Ancient Greece who believed in the gods and prayed for them for every single aspect of their daily lives, even the minor gods, the Romans believed the same thing. They would pray to their gods and give offerings to them in public spaces such as temples and even in prayer in their own homes.

Prior to conquering Greece, Rome was already a polytheistic country and race. Though there was already a rise in Judaism and Christianity, the vast majority were still polytheistic. However, upon reaching Greece and learning about their mythology and the stories of Zeus and the other Olympians, they adapted the stories of the Greeks and used them to influence their own mythological stories.

Due to them being in such close vicinities to each other, even before conquering Greece, Rome was slowly taking in bits of pieces of mythology from the citizens near the border or from those who would travel to Rome and would share stories about their deities. Rome then adopted these stories and changed some aspects, like their names, to better suit their existing practices and beliefs.

Roman mythology had three main gods: Jupiter, Juno, and Minerva. Jupiter is described the be the Sky God. It was believed that Jupiter would oversee all aspects of their lives and protect the Roman state. It was said that Roman military personnel would ask Jupiter for his blessing in battle and would later come back to the temple to thank him if they won. Juno is next. Juno is said to be the sister and wife of Jupiter. She is the goddess who oversees women and the aspects of their lives, such as their homes, livelihood, and childbirth. Lastly, there is Minerva. Minerva is the goddess of wisdom and craft. It is said that she watched over children and craftsmen such as blacksmiths, stonemasons, and carpenters.

Just by description alone, you can almost tell which parts of Greek Mythology these three main gods were based on. It was believed that Jupiter was based on the Greek god Zeus. The most obvious similarity is that they are both sky gods and are said to be all-powerful and all-seeing. Juno was probably adopted from Hera, based on how both goddesses are the sister and wife to the god of the sky in their respective cultures, but also they are both focused on women and women only. Lastly, Minerva. Knowing she is the goddess of wisdom already makes her connected to the Greek goddess Athena. However, Minerva and Athena do have some major differences. In Roman Mythology, Minerva had put herself in a self-imposed exile and did not ever have children or romantic partners. Athena, on the other hand, had the opposite experience. She mated with other gods and even mortal men.

When Rome conquered Greece, they had the Greek citizens adapt to their belief system as well, slowly cutting away at the stories of the original Twelve Olympians and other minor gods and goddesses in Greek Mythology.

Fun Fact:

Greek and Roman Mythology had quite a few differences, though very similar. In Greek Mythology, the gods and goddesses were seen as ethereal beings to worship and respect only. They believed that they could not possibly become gods and only lived to worship the gods and goddesses they knew of. Whereas in Roman Mythology, people use the gods and goddesses as inspiration for a way of living. This is because they believed that, once they died, they would enter an afterlife wherein they would have godly status.

Fun Fact:

Greek Myths put heavy emphasis on the physical appearances of the gods and goddesses, even the demigods and creatures. The Greek gods and goddesses were usually described to be physically strong and beautiful. Roman Myths rarely had a physical description of their gods and goddesses. If ever there was a description of the Roman gods and goddesses, they were described to be strong but not muscular like those of the Greeks.

Circle the Correct Word:

1. The **Romans/Turkish** conquered Greece in 146 BCE.

2. **Juno/Jupiter** is described the be the Sky God.

3. **Minerva/Juno** is said to be the sister and wife of Jupiter.

4. **Minerva/Mars** is the goddess of wisdom and craft.

5. Minerva has similarities to the Greek Goddess **Hera/Athena.**

Answers:

1. The **Romans** conquered Greece in 146 BCE.

2. **Jupiter** is described the be the Sky God.

3. **Juno** is said to be the sister and wife of Jupiter.

4. **Minerva** is the goddess of wisdom and craft.

5. Minerva has similarities to the Greek Goddess **Athena**.

THE RISE OF CHRISTIANITY

In 312 AD, Constantine, the Roman Emperor at the time known as "Constantine the Great," had been converted to Christianity. Over the years, Christianity rose in popularity throughout the Roman Empire, the Roman Empire itself being responsible for executing Jesus in Jerusalem, a city in Rome. At first, the Roman government frowned upon Christianity despite its rising popularity. Roman officials used to have those who believed in Christianity executed due to the whimsy of some government officials in Roman provinces. The Roman government believed that believing in anything but the Roman gods would be bad luck for their empire.

Prior to becoming the emperor of Rome, persecution of those who believed in Christianity had already been stopped, though many still looked down upon Christianity. That changed when, one day, Constantine was with his army on the Milvian Bridge, preparing for battle, when suddenly he and his men saw a holy cross formed in the sky. He did not really know the meaning behind the cross at the time and only recognized it as a symbol of Christianity. His conversion to Christianity and the many changes he made to the Romans' way of living did not happen instantly, but that moment was the catalyst for his intention to gain the freedom to worship and respect those who believed in Christianity.

Upon conversion to Christianity, Constantine the Great was baptized into Christianity by Eusebius of Nicomedia, an Arian priest, as claimed by many Arian historical figures. There are also claims made by the Catholic Church that it was Pope Sylvester I who baptized him into Catholicism. Scholars in the past, however, have refuted this claim. According to scholars, the Catholic Church made this claim in order to give Pope Sylvester I and the Catholic Church the credit for baptizing Constantine the Great.

In 313 AD, the Edict of Milan was decreed. This was a big deal to those who lived in the Roman Empire, especially to those who believed and practiced Christianity, because this was a decree that declared that the Christians within the Roman Empire would have the freedom to practice their beliefs openly without having to worry for their safety or their reputation. The decree states that everyone within the confines of the Roman Empire is to feel free to believe in any religion they want and to practice any religion they want in the freedom of their own homes or in public and without fear of judgment. Constantine had a heavy influence in the decreeing of the Edict of Milan. He also had a role in the creation of the Nicene Creed in 325 AD.

Christianity continued to rise over the years, slowly and surely erasing traces of the Greek and Roman Mythologies as religions, instead instilling Christianity. Christianity today is now one of the most common religions and belief systems in the world.

Fun Fact:

Christianity is known today as a religion. However, back when it first started, it was a movement. The early followers were called "Jews" and not "Christians." The word "Christian" wasn't used until the Jews settled in the Greek city of Antioch a few years after Jesus was crucified. It was here that the term "Christian" was used, the original Greek word meaning "Christianos" from the two Greek words "Christ" and "tian." "Christ" means "anointed," and "tian" means "little." In translation, Christian means "little anointed ones."

Fun Fact:

It is believed that Greek Philosophy heavily influenced Christianity. The early Christians used the way Greek philosophers taught and discussed the knowledge they had to spread information about Christianity and the story of Jesus and the word of God. Christians also used the knowledge of Greek Philosophy in a way to explain how their belief system works and why it should influence people for the better.

Reflection Questions

1. The early Christians were persecuted by the Roman Empire because of their beliefs. Do you see any parallels to this in today's modern age? Why or why not?

2. The early Christians used the way Greek Philosophers taught to spread information about Christianity. Do you think that this is still being done by Christians today? Why or why not?

GREEK MYTHOLOGY IN MODERN-DAY CULTURE

Greek Mythology was a culture and way of living for an entire civilization for centuries. And again, centuries later, it has been reduced to what we call "myths." Though it is no longer used as a basis for how people spend their days, it has never been forgotten. To this day, Greek Mythology, and the Greek language itself, still influences modern-day language, literature, and concepts.

In the English language alone, scholars and researchers have estimated that over 150,000 words have been derived from the Greek language. Words that start with the prefix "ph-" are most likely to have originated from the Greek language. Other words such as "micro," which means "small," and "demos," which means "people," also are derived from the ancient Greek language.

Words are not the only thing that has influenced the English language. Some expressions or figures of speech have also been adapted from Greek Mythology. A popular example would be the "Achilles' Heel." This is an expression that means "weakness." It was taken from the story of Achilles. Achilles was a warrior prince who fought in the Trojan War and died toward the end of it. It is said that, when he was a baby, his mother held him up by his heels and dipped him in the River Styx. The effect of his entire body being bathed in the River Styx made it impossible for him to be injured for long, making him almost invincible. However, because his heels were not touched by the River Styx, that part of his body was vulnerable, and his being injured at that exact spot was what led to his death. This story has been spread around and is now in most people's vernacular.

Stories of Greek Mythology continue to be spread today but, in a brand new medium. Just like in the time of Ancient Greece when the theater was rampant, and many plays were inspired by Greek Mythology, the film has become a new way to share the stories of the gods and goddesses. In 2004, the film, "Troy" was released. This was inspired by the story of Helen of Troy and the Trojan War. The 2010 film, "Clash of the Titans," was based on the story of Perseus, a demigod and one of Zeus's children with a mortal woman.

Now, in literature, many writers also take inspiration from the stories of Greek Mythology. Middle-Grade author, Rick Riordan, wrote his Percy Jackson series around the question, "what if the gods and goddesses really did exist and were still alive, but in secret?".

Romance authors have also taken inspiration from Greek Mythology. A very popular myth that has been adapted by many writers is the story of Hades and Persephone.

Persephone spends half of the year on Earth, bringing life and nature to the environment, and then spends the other half of the year in the Underworld with her husband, Hades, which is when the Earth turns to fall and winter. Books such as "Neon Gods" and "Lore Olympus" are popular adaptations of Hades and Persephone.

Greek Mythology has long been removed as a religion and belief system, yet its teachings, stories, characters, and elements still thrive today. Language, literature, and film are just some of what Greek Mythology and culture have influenced. There are many other aspects of today's daily living and culture that the Ancient Greeks are still influencing,

and it seems they will continue to do so for many years to come.

Fun Fact:

George R. R. Martin, a fantasy author, is most famous for his "A Song of Ice and Fire" series. In his series, he writes about his character, Robert Baratheon, who starts a war after his betrothed, Lyanna Stark, is taken captive by the royal prince, Rhaegar Targaryen. Though never confirmed by the author, it has been heavily theorized that this part of the story is inspired by Helen of Troy and the Trojan War

Fun Fact:

"The Song of Achilles" by Madeline Miller is a romance novel based on the story of Achilles and his friend, Patroclus. This book tells the story of Achilles's life from the perspective of Patroclus. Over the years, many believed that the two were actually secret lovers. Madeline Miller tells her version of this popular theory.

Discussion Questions

1. Greek Mythology and culture play a heavy influence on today's modern culture. What are the major ways in which modern culture was influenced?

2. Authors have taken to using Greek mythology stories as inspirations or basis for their own stories. Will literature continue to grow despite using existing stories?

CONCLUSION

"One thing that I know, that I know nothing. That is the source of my wisdom."

—*Socrates*

The rise of different cultures and organizations are just some of the reasons that Greek Mythology has been reduced to stories to be used for entertainment. Greek Mythology is not the only element of a great culture that is now known to be fiction. Many other cultures have gone through a similar fate. Roman Mythology, while most parts of it were based on Greek Mythology, was also a religion, now used to entertain many people. Myths from other European countries, African countries, and Asian countries are the same as well. Filipinos were polytheistic until the Spanish came and invaded the Philippines. The Americas, occupied by Native Americans, were mainly a polytheistic culture. When Christopher Columbus arrived in the

Americas, he brought Christianity with him, influencing Native Americans to convert, and resulting in the America we know today. This same thing has happened in many other countries and cultures, replacing one's existing religion with their own, but thankfully many have not forgotten these stories and have continued to pass them down for those in the future to enjoy and learn about.

Yes, though it has been centuries since Greek mythology was thought of as a religion, that does not erase it completely from history. Today, people are still learning about Greek Mythology, Roman Mythology, and many other myths, folklore, and legends from many other countries and cultures, and passing on their stories in many ways and forms—yes, mostly as a source of entertainment rather than the solemn aspect of life that it once was—but no one can ever erase the fact that Greek Mythology was once a religion and way of living that still captures the imagination of many and is as ever relevant.

Discussion Questions:

1. Scenes from Greek Mythology were painted on pottery pieces and later analyzed by scholars and archeologists. These scholars and archeologists were the ones who figured out what the scenes painted on the pottery were depicting. Since there were no actual descriptions, do you think these painted scenes were deciphered accurately?

2. Theater is a practice stemming from an ancient civilization. People of Ancient Greece used this as a means of worship. Today, it is used as a medium of entertainment. Do you think theater today is as important as it was back then?

3. Greek Mythology was originally a religion and way of living for those in Ancient Greece. Had the Roman Empire not invaded Greece, and Christianity had not risen and outlawed paganism, do you think worshipping the Greek gods and goddesses would still be a practice today?

4. Stories from Greek Mythology were used to reflect human behavior and be a guide for one's way of living, such as the story of Daedalus and Icarus. Do you think stories such as these still apply to the people living in today's modern age?

5. The works of Homer and Hesiod withstood the test of time. Their poems have been republished as books and are even being taught in schools. What does this say about their works and their importance?

6. Zeus is responsible for fathering many major figures in Greek Mythology. Some of these characters include Helen of Troy, Heracles, and Perseus. Do you think the stories of these characters in Greek Mythology would have played out differently if their father was any other god except for Zeus?

7. With Greece being conquered by multiple civilizations and empires and different religions and cultures replacing Ancient Greek practices, many Greek temples were destroyed. These Greek temples housed statues, sculptures, artworks, and pottery. Could today's

archeologists and researchers have been able to unearth more stories from Greek mythology had these temples not been destroyed?

8. Historical events such as the "Trojan War" was originally only a story from mythology until archeologists went and found proof of Troy and remnants of a great war. Do you think there are any other events from history that could have stemmed from mythology? Greek or otherwise?

True/False Questions:

1. **True or False**: Ancient Greeks believed that the first to appear in the world were the Titans. After the Titans, there were other creatures, such as the cyclops. The gods and goddesses of Olympus came next.

2. **True or False**: Pottery was the most accurate way of telling the stories of Greek Myths. This is commonly believed because those of Ancient Greece documented events and stories by painting on pottery. This is how archaeologists are able to determine what happened in the past.

3. **True or False:** Zeus was faithful to his wife, Hera. Zeus had many children, all of whom were conceived by him and Hera. Hera is the mother of all of Zeus's children.

4. **True or False:** After the battle against the Titans, Zeus, Poseidon, and Hades decided amongst themselves who would reign over what part of the Earth. Poseidon was the God of the Seas. Hades was the God of the Underworld. And Zeus was the God of

the Skies.

5. **True or False**: Artemis and Apollo are twins. Artemis is the Goddess of the Hunt. Apollo is the God of the Sun.

6. **True or False:** Athena and Ares are both considered to be Gods of War. Athena is the Goddess of War that focuses on battle. Ares is the God of War that focuses more on tactics and strategy.

7. **True or False:** Centaurs are known to be brutal and savage creatures. Chiron is the only centaur that was educated and mannered. One of Chiron's students was Achilles.

8. **True or False:** Roman Mythology has no connection to Greek Mythology whatsoever. There are no similarities between Greek Mythology and Roman Mythology. The Romans did not base their mythology off of the Greeks' at all.

True/False Answers:

1. True

2. False. Pottery was an inaccurate way of telling the stories of Greek Myths because it was open to interpretation.

3. False. Zeus was unfaithful to Hera and had many partners that resulted in many Greek characters being born. Hera did not consider any of Zeus's other offspring as her own child.

4. True.

5. True.

6. False. Athena focused more on tactics and strategy. Ares focused mainly on the battlefield and fighting.

7. True.

8. False. The Romans adapted many aspects of Greek Mythology and changed parts of it in order to better fit their culture and beliefs.

BIBLIOGRAPHY

- This picture shows Greek Pottery in a museum display. Many of the pieces shown have stories painted on them. "Greek Mythology" by Gary Lee Todd, Ph.D. is marked with CC0 1.0. To view the terms, visit https://creativecommons.org/publicdomain/zero/1.0/?ref=openverse.

- This is a statue of a Satyr on display in a museum's outdoor area." "Greek mythological creature" by ☺ Lee J Haywood is licensed under CC BY-SA 2.0. To view a copy of this license, visit https://creativecommons.org/licenses/by-sa/2.0/?ref=openverse.

- This is a statue of Pan the Satyr kept in Munich, Germany. "Pan and or Satyr, Munich Germany" by moonjazz is marked with Public Domain Mark 1.0. To view the terms, visit https://creativecommons.org/publicdomain/mark/1.0//?ref=openverse.

- This is a statue of Perseus, demigod and son of Zeus, holding the head of the gorgon, Medusa. "Perseus with the head of Medusa Marble Antonio Canova Italian carved in Rome 1804-06 CE Marble" by mharrsch is licensed under CC BY 2.0. To view a copy of this license, visit https://creativecommons.org/licenses/by/2.0/?ref=openverse.

- This is a statue of the goddess, Athena, made by Alan LeQuire. It is displayed in Nashville, Tennessee. This statue is a replica of the lost statue of Athena that used to be in the Parthenon. LeQuire used descriptions founded by archaeologists to create his work. "Athena -- The Parthenon Nashville (TN) July 2011" by Ron Cogswell is licensed under CC BY 2.0. To view a copy of this license, visit https://creativecommons.org/licenses/by/2.0/?ref=openverse

- The columns of this building are built to depict how the Titan, Atlas, is carrying the weight of the world on his shoulders. Atlas was sentenced to hold up the Earth for eternity. "Atlas" by Gabriela__F is licensed under CC BY-SA 2.0. To view a copy of this license, visit https://creativecommons.org/licenses/by-sa/2.0/?ref=openverse.

- This is a statue of the goddess, Aphrodite. This statue can be found in the Canakkale Archaeological Museum in Turkey. Late Hellenistic nude Aphrodite with snakes entwined around her left arm and left leg (symbol of Asklepios), found in the Tumulus of Dardanos, 2nd century B.C., Canakkale Archaeological Museum, Troy (Ilion), Turkey" by Following Hadrian is licensed under CC BY-SA 2.0. To view a copy of this license, visit https://creativecommons.org/licenses/by-sa/2.0/?ref=openverse.

About Us

At our core, we believe that history is more than just a subject to be learned. It's an experience to be had.

Our mission is to educate and inspire the next generation by providing them with a window into the fascinating and often surprising world of the past. We want to help young people make sense of the complexities of history and understand the lessons it has to offer.

By creating unforgettable encounters with relics of the past, we hope to ignite a lifelong passion for learning and discovery.

Thank you,